WHAT DOES *She* REALLY WANT

Everything you want to know
to win your wife's heart

I0176906

MAHESH
KRISHNAMURTHY

notionpress
.com

INDIA · SINGAPORE · MALAYSIA

Notion Press

Old No. 38, New No. 6
McNichols Road, Chetpet
Chennai - 600 031

First Published by Notion Press 2019
Copyright © Mahesh Krishnamurthy 2019
All Rights Reserved.

ISBN 978-1-7321901-3-9

Dedication and Prayer

I dedicate this book to my dear friend Rajendra for whom I really penned down the content of this book.

I would also like to dedicate this book to my wife who has stood by me, taking all the pressure of my presence in her life. It is her presence which has made me understand what she really wants that inspired me to dwell deeper.

My daughter is the next in line who also gets asked by people who know me; how do you tolerate this man! I dedicate this book to her.

I have come a long way in knowing how I can live with these two women in my life and be happy.

– Mahesh Krishnamurthy

Contents

Foreword

Of Her, For Her!

A recent KPMG report sizes the Indian wedding market to be around $40–50 billion in size, with an annual growth rate of 25–30%. Despite the high-involvement events that weddings are, 'settling down' in a marriage is the most underestimated transition that mankind acknowledges.

Marriage is perhaps the perfect point for 'moment of truth' to emerge; where one decides to open one's space of completeness to envelope and include the partner's sense of self. Arguably, opening of a space, could make one feel 'vulnerable' or exposed, or could serve as opportunity to learn from each other and grow together in unison!

Be it in corporate corridors or academic meetings, there is increasing attention to gender-sensitivity deliberations all of which attempt to focus on 'Her,' albeit with differing degree of success. It is often amusing to witness animated, well prepared keynote addresses that manage to craft a value-driven prescription to 'Understand Her.'

As a daughter, mother and more importantly a woman I acknowledge we can be difficult to decode at times, even for the most prepared man. We seek absolute honesty yet expect you to be mysterious to 'keep the fire burning'; we seek predictability yet love countless surprises from you. We want a friend to confide in sans judgment yet need our spa-ce to be just with ourselves. We like to pay our own bills yet like to be spoilt to no end from you. While this concoction of contradictions could be puzzling, we have our own innate ways to 'signal' to you, what we are about. Decoding that script needs no cryptology, but an active sense of being present to everything that is 'Her.'

In the pages that follow, Mahesh shares an insightful account punctuated with heart-warming personal anecdotes. The words in this narrative spell humility of a seeker, yet the state of grandeur to want to make an ongoing difference to lives. Each chapter represents active ingredients that go into cooking up a soulful recipe for life in a relationship. The beauty of this work is the focus on the 'process of preparation' and not on the perfect-taste of what the outcome is to be like!

Every reader is deeply fortunate to have this work crafted for him in the words of Mahesh; here's wishing each of us happy beginnings, each day!

Much Love,

– Dr. Smitha Sarma Ranganathan

Brand Communication Specialist

Preface

My friend Rajendra was getting married. Despite our telling and signaling him in different ways, we found that he couldn't come around to accept the fact that he was good looking. His self worth and self respect simply was too heavy to rise.

So, I thought the best gift I could present to him will be some words which he can go back to, so that, in the times when none of us are available with him, he can find our words to comfort and guide him.

This is the reason this book took shape. This book has my experience of counseling and guiding thousands of individual men, women and couples successfully.

I pray this book will be of help to every person who is getting married to know how he must be and how he must be there for his wife.

Mahesh Krishnamurthy

Mahesh Krishnamurthy

Chapter - 1

Trust

Trust is the glue of life. It's the most essential ingredient in effective communication. It's the foundation principle that holds all relationships.

– Stephen Covey

A relationship between a man and a woman depends on several unspoken expectations from the woman. We are specifically discussing this topic because men more than often, find convenient ways to navigate through situations as it is seemingly easier and less stressful. Women usually take the trusted path, even if it means that they have to face some challenges and hardships on the way. Honesty and transparency are two qualities that women expect their men to exhibit. Are you honest and transparent with your wife? How can you win your wife's trust? How can you get your wife to believe in you?

Trust doesn't increase by Sharing everything with your wife

I met a Swamiji who once told me; do not share all information with your wife, especially about finances. Some matters must be kept close to your chest. Play it safe. It does not mean she won't trust you! Women are emotional. Do not share financial matters with them.

I am not sure whether to trust this information shared by the Swamiji or not. Because the Swamiji was never married. So, how do we deal with this information?

Well, this is what I learnt from experienced people.

Let Life Be an Open Book

Between you and your wife, let life be an open book. What does this mean? You don't have to go on reporting to your wife about everything that is happening in your life! That's outrageous. That is a sign that you are mesmerised by something in your wife that's caught your attention and you are not able to let go of it. And that is why you want to please her every time so that you can have more and more of her.

Honesty shows on your face.
Trust builds over time.

The above statement about being the open book means that all matters about you must be accessible to your wife. There must be nothing hidden. Trust does not come from sharing everything with your wife. However, there are some information that are accessible, yet not discussed. For example; finances. This is because, when hard times come, man will take some measures to make money available at home for the house to run. A woman, who may be overtly sensitive, immature and inexperienced in these matters, may cast doubt and aspersions about her man's ways and may weaken his resolve to keep the family afloat during bad financial times.

Winning Your Wife's Trust

It is not important to share everything with your wife to prove to her that you are honest with her and trustworthy. What is important is how you win her trust. It is obvious from the countless examples we have around us that you cannot win the trust of your woman through conceit or deceitful ways. Honesty shows on your face. Trust builds over time.

A woman usually feels her way through. She judges less but accepts more of how things are. That way she keeps her heart clean. However, her mind is a mess because of the confusion that erupts in her when a man says something, means something else and does something entirely different. This is where all hell breaks loose.

How Women Perceive Honesty

What it means to be honest with your wife is simply like this. If you say a certain thing, be clear what you mean when you communicate with her. Further, act on it. When you think, it shows on your face. When you speak, you express your thinking. And when you act, it must all fall in line. That, to a woman is honesty.

You might be honest. But, if you said something, and did not act on it, it doesn't measure up to being honest with her. You could very easily let a women down by simply not acting on what you spoke about with her.

Next time you speak with your woman, be careful about what words come out of your mouth because, she is listening very intently. She trusts you. You cannot make your wife happy by just holding her hands and taking her to a movie! Being practically honest is one sure way of winning your place in her heart.

Chapter - 2

Be Smart

*When a wife has a good husband, it is easily seen on
her face.*

– Johann Wolfgang Von Goethe

Are you the smart guy your wife is looking for in you? Smartness
in a man makes the woman feel more sensuous. Being smart
is one of the traits a woman wishes her man to possess. Being
smart is not like a game of chess. Don't think too much. Be
yourself.

Have you taken your mother Saree shopping?

Did you know, when you are marrying a woman, she
silently is wishing her man to be superman? Have you ever
taken your mother or your aunts saree shopping? I Have.

Many women, especially my aunts ask for saree colour
combinations that have never been made. I wonder why
the weavers never dreamt of such combinations! Likewise, a
woman expects traits in a man that are difficult to find.

Be Smart

Smartness has to do with quick and intelligent decision making. It's about taking charge of a situation. If you are slow and take time to clear the fog in your mind, then, your wife is not the one to appreciate you.

Women take pride in showcasing their smart husbands just like men like to showcase their beautiful women. When you are smart, you showcase your intelligence through your actions. You are very clear about where and how you will showcase your intelligence. When you are smart and sensitive, it is a killer combination. Any woman would embrace with open arms, her man who is smart and sensitive.

Don't Try to Be Smart

This chapter is for men who are getting married or, are newly married. A caution to married men – Please do not woo other women after reading this chapter. Women are smarter than men. They know your moves even as you are thinking. So, don't think you can outsmart women. What I write is backed by my experience with working with literally thousands of married couples and courting partners.

Your Smartness Is for Your Family First

Many men whom I have seen are smart when they are in the company of their friends or in a social gathering but, are very serious and unromantic when they are with their spouse! I don't get it. Why are you so dry with your spouse? Your wife will be the first one who will appreciate your smartness, not an outsider. The equation between a man and his woman are good when both contribute to the relationship with sensitivity and sensibly.

Joke Once in a While

Being smart also means to be humorous. Don't be too serious with life. When you are serious, it's boring. Believe me, women don't like their man to be boring. You are serious when its business! When you are working, you are serious. She understands that. However, when work is done and you are with her, then, break the silence by adding some fun into your life. I am not asking you to make your wife laugh! Be spontaneous.

The Frowning Lady

Here is an example; We were driving home after work. One man, overtook us from the wrong side and gave me a dirty look as if I was on the wrong side. My wife and I were both startled by his behaviour, but we were quick to let it pass. I continued driving and I turned into a street which we always take to reach home because it is less crowded. At this time of the day, we get to see a rather serious looking woman on a bicycle. She frowns upon anyone who travels in a 4-wheeler. So, my wife and I were driving on that street and we saw her cycling.

I practice selective amnesia which means, I choose not to remember what's unimportant. This includes the woman who was cycling at that time.

So, when we saw the woman, I spontaneously joked; If this woman stops me and accuses me saying; you were staring at me. I, with my memory loss would ask her; when? That would infuriate her even more. And we both burst out laughing. It was such a funny moment.

Sometimes, you are the funniest topic to discuss. Laugh at yourself. Being able to laugh at yourself shows that you are smart. That's the best way to keep your mood light. Unconsciously you will fill the air with love.

Don't Look for Feedback

You are foolish if you look for approval for your behaviour in your wife. Be yourself, but don't be unreal. Obsessed men always look for approval so they feel secure. Women are not happy with approval seeking men. When you are yourself, you are real. You are being natural. That's okay. Being serious is not being you. Sometimes, women like the feeling of being around you and enjoy the moment. Women feel more sensuous when they're around their smart man. Seeking approval of any kind can turn them off.

I don't what to overwhelm you with overloaded instructions. Observe yourself outside of home. Observe yourself, the strong and smart decision maker. See how many people appreciate you for the decisions you take, for your smartness and wit. You just need to be that self with your wife. It's that simple. Just that, don't try to make her happy. Be happy and she'll be happy too. You just remember that women feel more sensuous when their man is smart.

Chapter - 3

What Do Women Really Want?

When you run through the quotes on what a woman wants, you will exhaust all the quotes and still not find the one you are looking for.

– Mahesh Krishnamurthy

You can tell a man is fallen for his woman when he tells you – I want to understand her. Women so wish that their man understand them, not know them. Women are romantic. A man can never understand a woman. This is because women are always experimenting. Women are dynamic. They are always finding out ways of romanticising with their man. If you want to know what your woman really wants, you need to be smart, you need to see under the cover to find the pieces of the puzzle.

Women derive their joy from having their man to discover what she is communicating with him. If you are a man who has fallen for your woman, get up. This is just the beginning of the maze. Find out what the romantic woman really wants.

What Does My Woman Really Want!

Men often get confused with what women really want. The biggest piece of the puzzle is to understand what a woman wants. Women get so overwhelmed with their role as the daughter-in-law, wife, mother, sister-in-law and so on that the lack of their man's support gets them to become frustrated. That's when she loses her cool and she begins to test her man. The man is often insensitive and does not put the pieces of the puzzle together to understand what his woman is actually asking. Here are some situations for you to know what your woman might be asking of you and what is her real intention.

Can You Get That Bottle from the Shelf?

Many a times, a woman asks her man to get a certain container from the kitchen shelf. It is not that she cannot reach it! The man walks in and realises that she can take it herself. An argument begins because her demand was unrealistic. When she asked, you probably were reading something on your mobile or glued to your seat watching television.

You are right. Your wife was indeed able to reach the container from the kitchen shelf. Did you realise what she was up to? While cooking, your wife probably felt romantic and wanted your company in the kitchen. She uses techniques like these to draw you into the kitchen and have you beside her. If you reacted, then, this was a game gone sour for her.

Can You Buy Some Groceries on Your Way Home?

Men have placed themselves high up on the pyramid and they believe, without them nothing can happen. So, when a man walks out of his office, he believes finally, he can get back to his den. Just then, his wife calls him and asks him to purchase groceries from the market. The thought makes him even more tired. He feels famished. He picks up the groceries comes home alright but, he missed the plot altogether. Did you realise that your wife was just romanticising?

Women are romantic and put most of their energies in romanticising their environment.

The Romantic Woman

Women are romantic and put most of their energies in romanticising their environment. Women are very passionate about their home and their surroundings. They want to keep experimenting. In this scenario, your woman was excited that you were coming home. So, she thought of making something exciting to eat at dinner and that's how the shopping list emerged in her mind. Well, if you argued with her asking; couldn't you get the groceries yourself? What have you been doing all day? Why do you ask me to stop and shop for groceries? I'm already so tired from the day's work. You just poured water on all of her excitement.

The Romantic Man

Its not that only women are romantic! Men are also equally romantic. More than often, men turn naughty and their romanticism comes to a conclusion very quickly.

I remember I was once at a shopping mall. I was waiting for my wife. So, I positioned myself on the mezzanine floor so that I could see the vast central area of the ground floor. Several people were criss-crossing walking their path. My attention caught a man who was hiding behind a pillar. He sported a broad smile. I saw him tip toe from one pillar to another. He must have been in his 50's. Then, I saw this lady enter the central area. She had noticed him and was smiling too. That's when I realised that the romantic man that he was, he was trying to surprise his woman. It was such a romantic sight to see.

I Want You to Buy Me a Diamond Necklace

This demand for a diamond necklace can drive a man's throat dry. But, yes, women can demand such things off her man. However, it is important for us men to understand the puzzle behind the demand. What is your wife really asking for?

If there's anything a women demands, it's her man's attention. Women rarely demand gold and jewellery. You are now thinking, nah! Yes, women do like gold and stones studded in their ornaments. However, they get satisfied very easily provided the man knows the know how.

Mostly, women demand for expensive purchases from their man only as a gesture to get his attention and his time with her. If you don't get it, you'd probably wipe sweat off your forehead or swipe your credit card. Either way, you lost the plot. Your wife will resign with hurt thinking, why doesn't he get it!

The Home She Has Decorated

Women like to keep their home and their relationship both renewed and refreshed. So, they keep doing things to the house and to their relationship with their partner so that they both get a face-lift quite often. This includes making changes to oneself, making changes in the arrangement of artefacts or showcase items, a re-arrangement of furniture or minor additions such as adding a fruit basket or an arrangement of flowers on the dining table.

Men are usually oblivious to such changes. Their gaze does not catch the subtle but obvious changes in the setting. A woman's mood awakens when her man is able to call out the changes and appreciate her and her ingenuity.

> **Women like to keep their home and their relationship both renewed and refreshed.**

There are literally countless ways that a woman will find to experiment with so that she can keep her relationship with you exciting. Live up to her excitement and the two of you will have the best time of your life. Marriage is all about keeping your batteries renewed from time to time. Nothing really ends when you marry the person you chose as your life partner. The game has just begun.

Chapter - 4

Happiness Is a Choice

Happiness is not something readymade.
It comes from your own actions.

– Dalai Lama

Chetan is a civil services officer working with the Indian Government. He is a very happy, smart, witty, loving and a gentle soul. He is married and has two children. Chetan's wife is also a civil services officer working with the Indian Government. They are both extremely dedicated to their jobs. That hasn't stopped him from retaining his childlike humour, his charismatic smile and character, something that is rare to see. When Chetan visited Bangalore, I went to see him. His expression after seeing the trees in Bangalore was something that will stay in my mind. His eyes widened and smile broadened. He said; the trees here are so alive and healthy. They look so happy. Chetan's family is a happy family. They care for one another. Living happily for them is a choice they have made.

Living Happily Is Not the Same as...

Couples today find it difficult to find happiness in their relationship. They in turn derive pleasure from watching movies, dining out and splurging on online shopping and in malls. Living happily and enjoying pleasures are two entirely different ends of the spectrum. Enjoying pleasures has got to do everything with me...me...me...me...me, while living happily is about making a difference to other people's lives. Driving the point home, learn how you can live happily with your spouse.

> **Women are like little children.**
> **They want to be free and yet,**
> **when they turn around to see,**
> **they want to make sure that**
> **you are watching over them.**

Show Her You're There for Her

What Chetan did is an example for most men to imbibe into their marriage. Chetan not only was an excellent husband and father, what mattered was, what he did to demonstrate that he cared.

On Sundays Chetan made some simple dishes for breakfast while his wife would wake up the kids and get them ready for the day. One day, As his wife was in the kitchen, preparing dinner, Chetan quietly walked in and started doing the dishes. You doesn't have to announce that you care. When you know certain chores have to be done, go do it, whether it is doing dishes or spreading the clothes to dry on the clothesline. How on earth are you going to let your wife know that you are there for her? This is how she feels your love for her. What did you do last that demonstrated that you care?

Get to Know Each Other

I remember a couple came to consult me. The wife had introduced her husband as a charming, jovial and witty personality. They had been married for a good 10 years, it seemed. I accept every character at face value. Only when I do a Nadi Pariksha do I get to know the correct picture.

So, I investigated and evaluated his physical, mental and emotional health with the help of Ayurvedic pulse diagnosis. I shared with him that he was a deeply hurt and lonely person. This came as a shock to his wife. He gently nodded his head in acceptance with a sad smile. He held his sorrows deep within himself. His wife had not seen through those eyes. One needs to be sensitive to see beyond the smile, listen through the sentences spoken and sense through the air. That's when you participate in a relationship. Care is about being sensitive to your partner intuitively.

Don't Blame One Another

Do you remember your kiddy days? Do you remember how you played? When adults were not around, we sorted out issues by ourselves. We didn't blame one another. We lived in the solution and not in the problem. Present day kids are different though!

When you have a challenge, don't blame each other. Live in the solution. Blaming each other and pulling each other's families into your fight is not difficult. Your relationship with your wife will be scarred for life. The challenge is to live in the solution. Believe me, the rewards you get from taking on such challenges together is worth a lifetime. When you work together towards the solution, bonds strengthen, love expands, confidence between each other enhances and you laugh together more.

Listen Intentionally

This part is especially for men. When your wife is speaking, put your phone down and listen to her intentionally. Eye contact with your wife when she is speaking with you is necessary for communication to happen. What she says is not important. The subject she's discussing with you might be boring. She also knows that. But what she wants is eye contact and communication. Women get frustrated when their man does not make eye contact when she is speaking with him.

By watching the phone when she's speaking with you, you just demonstrated who's important and who's not. There are no two ways to it. Next time your wife speaks with you, put the phone down and listen to her intentionally. It goes a long way in building a relationship.

Love Naturally

When you love, it shows. Loving your spouse is not the same as hanging around with her all the time. That's possessiveness.

Possessiveness is toxic. Ask any woman, she'll want to run away to freedom from her possessive partner. Love is freedom. When you love your spouse, you are there for her when she needs you. You support her unconditionally. At the same time, you also let her know when she's not right.

Women are like little children. They want freedom and yet, when they turn around, they want to make sure that you are watching over them.

Living happily is all about feeling your way around in life. You have to be sensitive, cautious and sensible while communicating with your spouse. Keep your heart open and feel the energy around you when your spouse is around. You'll then know how to communicate with your spouse so that both live happily with each other.

Marriage is a jigsaw puzzle that you need to solve every time. And the puzzles keep changing. Make sure you enjoy your life as you solve the puzzle.

Chapter - 5

Be Humorous

Humour breaks down boundaries, it topples our self-importance, it connects people, and because it engages and entertains, it ultimately enlightens.

– John Agard

Humour is such a mood elevator that it can turn situations from being sad to happy. I remember when we were holidaying in a resort, two people came to visit the resort owners. They were partners of a sprawling business. Their high pressure jobs wouldn't function if they had to throw their tempers in. They instead turned witty. Each one was cracking witty humourous jokes on the other. I asked one of them; is it your high pressure job that's making you crack these witty jokes? He agreed. Marriage too can go through high pressure situations. When you are witty instead of being satirical, you'll turn your relationship into an ocean of love and joy.

Love is the only potion to live by.
Every other emotion is a poison

**that weakens you little by little
until you are left with nothing.**

Use witty humour when you are stressed.

Jivan (name changed) and his wife had an arranged marriage. Their parents were friends and that his how the alliance happened.

Soon after marriage, Jivan realised that his mother and wife did not get along well. They were satirical with each other. So, he decided to separate the two of them by a floor. His parents stayed in the ground floor while he stayed on the first floor with his wife. Life began with his wife. Everything was okay for Jivan until reality struck to the couple that they are physically not capable of bearing children of their own. Stress began to brew between them.

Jivan was quick to smell the stress and brought out the wit in him to lighten the air. His wife too reciprocated to his witty humour equally. They made their life more humorous.

A few years later Jivan and his wife adopted a daughter Kshama, who learnt from her parents to be witty. Today, the family is living humorously. Jivan and his wife have been married for close to two decades. Whenever our families meet, humour is how we communicate with each other.

Love Is the Only Potion

Love is the only potion to live by. Every other emotion is a poison that weakens you little by little until you are left with nothing. Loving is natural. It's who you really are. Do you remember holding an infant in your hands? What do you feel like? Happy? Loved? Do you know that is what the little child is doing to you? That child is being love. When you get into a room full of love, you'll become quiet and want to be love too. That is the power of love. Well, let me remind you that this is what you did to your parents too. When you were an infant, you too were love. Now that you have changed, you need lessons to get back to being love. It's something like needing a GPS to get back home.

Be Quick Witted Naturally

We all have a natural sense of humour. Our humour is hidden when we are scared. A newly married man often get perturbed by what his wife will think of him. This causes him to be extremely cautious of his behaviour. I am telling you, be yourself. Let your wife know you. You did not murder anyone or jump the prison wall! So, stop being so serious.

Good witty humour is a sign of your intelligence. When you are humorous, you are also often spontaneous. Spontaneity is also an indicator of your connectedness with your inner core. Your innermost being, your reality is love, joy, peace and humour. Sometimes you do crack sick jokes! Just don't bother. However bad you might be at jokes, you'll get better with practice.

Don't Be Serious

Partners often take life too seriously. Don't be serious. Seriousness is the beginning of a sick mind. A sick mind produces a sick body. People who have witty humour often have less or no illnesses to complain about. People who take life too seriously are always complaining about one thing or the other.

Marriage is two mirrors coming together to reflect each other. Your behaviour and expressions are opportunities for your partner to respond to and vice versa. How well you did will depend on what responses you get from your partner. Just make sure every response from you and your partner are worth a lifetime of humorous entertainment and happiness.

Chapter - 6

Be Passionate

Passion is energy. Feel the power that comes from focussing on what excites you.

– Oprah Winfrey

Peter (name changed) and his wife came to me a few days ago. Peter had read about spirituality. He was reading about how you can claim your freedom. Peter was married. In the process of following the author who had written the text, Peter distanced himself from his wife. He became less intrusive and less involved when his wife expressed herself emotionally. He also taught his wife how she can stay unaffected. However, what he practiced did not lead him to freedom. Somewhere he felt stuck, but, he couldn't find out. His wife was going into depression. She felt worthless because Peter had stopped involving himself in her affairs. Their marriage was dry with no passion. Peter learnt the 3 steps to increase passion in relationship. Their marriage is back on track with freedom and passion.

What Does It Mean to Be Passionate in Your Relationship?

Passion between two people increases through several intentionally strong verbal or non-verbal actions. Passion does not mean lust. When you are passionate with your wife, you will do a few things that will ignite love in the air. Here are a few ways you can increase passion in your relationship so that you can ignite love in-between.

Passion means to be in synchronicity with your partner

Be Blind for the Right Reasons

Love is blind. Be blind for the right reasons. More than often, I have seen people being blindly in love with a partner. It is only after marriage that they realise what they have got themselves into. And they wonder why they even committed themselves into that relationship.

One of the best ways to increase passion in relationship is to love unconditionally. When you love, you become less intrusive. I remember an instance when a friend of mine was with his wife in a temple. At that time, the priest was offering devotees mudra-dharane, a religious practice of using 'Mudras' (dyes) usually made of gold or copper that are heated on a coal fire and stamped on the body.

My friend is opposed to this practice. He believes it is an inhuman practice whereas his wife believes it is not only a religious practice, but also has health benefits to it.

On that day, my friend and I were sitting in meditation in front of the deity. We were immersed in love. His wife returned after partaking Darshan and asked my friend whether she can take mudra-dharana. He not only consented to her request, he also accompanied her and watched, while still immersed in love, as she got her mudra-dharana done.

When you are in love, you are less intrusive

Appreciate Your Partner Often

We all do several things everyday. Many of the tasks we take on, are accomplished in different ways. Sometimes, the method we use are unique to us and unusual at times. Whenever your wife uses an unusual method that throws a different perspective of how differently a task can be accomplished, appreciate her. Appreciation brings in new life into us. We all like appreciate when it comes. Appreciating your partner usually brings the two of you closer to each other. Appreciation does increase passion in your relationship.

Never fake your appreciation. You must not want to be close to your partner. You will be close to your partner when you are genuine with your partner. More than often, your partner will get to know when you are faking it. So, be careful.

One person brought his wife to me for consultation because she had headaches. My diagnosis through Nadi Pariksha revealed that it was lack of appreciation that caused her frustration which resulted in her headache. This man was busy creating assets for his wife and daughter while she had become impatient waiting for his appreciation.

Women will be better of re-claiming their freedom instead of waiting for appreciation.

Leave Her Alone When She Needs It

More often, we men tend to dig into our spouse's sadness. If you haven't yet learnt, then, here it is. When your wife is upset, just be there with her but, don't speak a word. Don't even breathe loudly. Just be there. You can leave her alone only if she wants you to. Don't appreciate your wife when she is not in the best of her moods. It will boomerang in a way you would've least expected.

A woman feels more comfortable when her man is around her. More so, when she is upset. She doesn't need your understanding or care. She just wants you to be there for her when she needs you. That only she can tell when she needs you and when she doesn't.

You can be a great companion to your partner when you stop understanding her and yet trust her. Appreciate her when she has cooked a meal, achieved a goal or accomplished a task. Before I complete, I'd like to say that men look for more appreciation than women. Men latch on to the person who appreciates them as if they are getting a carton of dark chocolate.

Chapter - 7

Never Compromise

When you are saying "Yes" to others, make sure you're not saying "No" to yourself.

– Paulo Coelho

A lady came in for a consultation the other day. I performed her Nadi Pariksha. I made a list of the symptoms she had and also the root cause of all of these symptoms. When I read out the symptoms, she was definitely overwhelmed because she had ignored most of the symptoms which were lingering in her. The root cause was what caught her attention and she reflected. She had a frozen shoulder, fatty liver disease and high fasting blood sugars. The root cause of her condition were the compromises she had made with her husband. She had to even compromise her self worth.

What went wrong was that she had begun to sacrifice her small desires and aspirations for her husband, but that did nothing to their relationship. Then, the only choice she had was to either walk out of the marriage or compromise. She even compromised with her self worth.

**Compromise is a ransom you
pay to retain something
you value.**

Compromise Is a Ransom You Pay

In a relationship between two people, where interaction is the key method of communication, one must never compromise. Compromise means to give away what you cherish in order to save something. It's not a choice. Compromise is a ransom you pay to retain something you value. When a man or a woman compromises in a relationship, there cannot be peace between them. There can be no harmony. The relationship will rest on threads of fire which will flareup every now and then. When you are in love, you sacrifice. You also decide what you will sacrifice and what you will sacrifice for. A sacrifice happens when you let go with love and for love, not for a person. There's great value in sacrifice.

**Sacrifice is when you let go
with love and for love**

You Need to Choose When to Sacrifice

I suggest every person reading this chapter to never compromise in their lives. Compromise is not worth it. When you compromise, it is like walking naked. It's, being bare, with nothing to secure yourself with. Compromise depletes you.

Sacrifice always enhances your value. There's happiness and joy in sacrifice. Let me give you an example; I was writing this chapter a while ago when my son woke up and walked up to me. He likes to sit on my lap and laze for a while before he goes on to brush his teeth. Even though writing is both necessary and important for me, I decided to put the laptop aside and let him sit on my lap for whatever time he wanted to. This bonding between us is invaluable. It enhances love between us. The writing can then wait for that many more minutes.

Now, let us look at an example of compromise. Roma gets married. She is disciplined and time bound. Her husband Rishab is calm, not rushed and doesn't bother being a few minutes late. Roma believes in valuing her's as well as others' time. Rishab doesn't bother much about value. Rishab takes his own time. Now Roma has a choice of either continuing valuing her time and schedules or giving into Rishab's indiscipline and let go of her schedules for his sake. If she gives into Rishab's indiscipline, that would be a compromise.

Being in Balance

When you are married to a person who does not believe in discipline or value for time, and one who decides to compromise, choose to be okay with that. However, choose to be disciplined without taunting your partner. That's where your happiness lies. It is necessary for each person to choose their timeline to get to the realisation that compromise depletes their life. Telling them won't help.

It might actually create more friction than produce results. Marriage is an arrangement of opposites of not only the sexes but also of mental attitudes and attributes. What's common is the love that blooms between them. When you are aware, you will sacrifice your indiscipline for love to blossom and spread.

Chapter - 8

Family Time Is Important

If you want your children to turn out well, spend
twice as much time with them and half
as much money.

– Abigail Van Buren

A woman expects her man to help those in need. When a man is sensitive to his environment and helps the needy, knowingly or unknowingly, he just touched her heart. However, women can be very complicated at times. If the person he helped is a man, that's okay. If whom he helped is a woman, she is all ears to what is happening. She can get cautious and jealous. But a woman rarely assumes. Her intuition is very strong and she never misses. While helping others is good, you need to absorb a few realities of life – family time is important, friendships are forever but…, help ever – hurt never, love all – serve all and live at the edge of attachment – detachment.

When You Help a Person...

It is important for you to know when to help a person and when to back off. People can get very dependant on you if you did not know when to back off. Furthermore, they grow their tentacles into your family and rob you of your family time.

One of the main reasons why your woman might not take a liking to your service to others is, when your help for others eats into her family time with you. Your family time must not be compromised for anything.

Family Time Is Important

Sometimes, help is needed urgently. Your woman understands that! But, don't be out every Sunday and every other day to help people. It's good to help people on scheduled days. I personally know several people who conduct free medical camps on Sundays. That's a huge service they are doing to humanity. However, your wife is as important a person and she needs your time too. Your wife might not need food packets or medicine supplies. However, she does need love and care and time to spend with you and interact with you. That is a priority you must count into your days when you are helping others. But, never try to understand her when you mess with the time you promised her.

No matter how much time you spend outside serving others, and no matter how tired you get, make sure you have some moments for family time. Its like your main door. Before you open the door to step out, spend time with your woman. And when you return home from work, shut the door to the outside world so that you can spend time with your family. Such a habit is very healthy.

Friendships Are Forever

I have a few friends who can do anything for me and I will stretch to any extent to help them. It's not an understanding! It's given that in any situation that demands my presence, I'll be there. There are these times when our first priority will become a friend or when we are helping someone who is not even known to you. In such times, it is important to focus on your immediate environment rather than think of home. Service to the nation is as important as family time. It's paradoxical at times. Only a person who has a partner must decide which must take precedence over what.

Help Ever – Hurt Never

This is a famous quote given by Sathya Sai Baba for people to follow. And it must be applied first at home. Most of us are kind to people outside of home and release all our emotional garbage at ho me as if home was a garbage bin. If you really want to help the needy, do it. However, keep in mind that your home is where your heart is and you must protect, nurture and nourish your home as much as you are nurturing the helpless and the wounded.

Love All – Serve All

I know several families where the woman is not familiar with the Sai Baba devotees. She is okay with her husband rushing off to work on weekdays. However, even on weekends, she doesn't have him. He is rushing off to love all and serve all. Sathya Sai Baba never said leave home and love others! All of your actions must begin at home.

It is easy to practice help ever-hurt never and love all – serve all outside. When you help the needy, those people will thank you immensely and your pride will intoxicate your head and you will feel invincible. At home, no matter how much you try to love and serve and help and not hurt, they don't give up the taunts and sarcasm. This is your real battle ground. Not the world outside. If you can master your emotions at home, you won.

Attachment – Detachment

The world is like a tug of war. Your heart pulls one side to love and to help the needy, to serve, while the mind pulls you in an entirely different direction to indulge in attachments, pleasures and self importance.

Your heart know only to love. That is the best place to be. However, the mind interferes and manipulates the feelings and makes a mess out of the situation.

Beware of the Mind

Whatever help you render to society, make sure you are not attached to the congregation of people with whom you go out to help. What are you helping for? Helping others is the best way to take your mind out of yourself and put it in your heart so that you can work for the society. At the same time, fill your mind and mouth with God's holy name so that you do not get to the arrogance of "I did this." Practice – all work is God's work.

Also, do not be attached to the words people speak including that of your woman. Don't spend your time feeling hurt. She as well as others, have a right to their perception and judgment. It has nothing to do with you. You just need to have your head in the forest (in God) and hands ready to serve.

Your woman will be happy when you understand – when to help the needy and when you know to back off from all that and give time to the family. Family time is important. She is okay with your attitude of help ever-hurt never, but she will try to poke a needle at you at times just to see if you react. Watch it. If you do, she will be quick to point out saying; is this the same way you behave with others? And you will be tongue tied.

She also knows that you want to love all and serve all. But, make sure you don't embrace everyone and keep them in your mind. Allow God to work through you. That way you too will be filled with God's love. When God's love fills your heart, love is what will flow through you, even at home.

And finally, the only attachment you need is to your Inner God. That's the only connection which must never get strained.

Chapter - 9

Boost Your Self Respect

To be yourself in a world that is constantly trying to make you something else is the greatest accomplishment.

– Ralph Waldo Emerson

It is important to have a high sense of self respect. When your presence and conduct exhibits your self respect, people respect you too. However, when you do not maintain your self respect, you demand respect or feel hurt when someone doesn't respect you. Self respect is just a reflection. When you respect yourself, you earn respect from others. It just comes back to you. So, today, let's understand, how you can boost your self respect in just 3 steps.

How Does a Lack of Self Respect Affect Your Health?

A lack of self respect can create a feeling of guilt in you. Guilt occurs from dishonouring words that you have spoken. The words you speak are your own. You own them. When you do not follow what you have spoken, you dishonour your own words. This creates guilt in you. Guilt further causes you to seek acceptance and appreciation from the world around you.

Guilt affects your lungs. When you harbour feelings of guilt in you, your lungs partially collapse resulting in reduced intake and absorption of oxygen. This progressively causes restlessness, anxiety and depression. It may also affect of your liver and kidney function, thereby causing symptoms of blood pressure and fatty liver disease.

Boost your self respect by observing your thinking.

For so many years, you have been following the ways of the mind. You have been thinking that it's okay to not be disciplined, It's okay to sleep on ideas that otherwise could have changed your life. And, it's okay to browse social media. On the whole, you have thought it's okay to be the way the mind directs. Well! Here is a piece of truth for you. If you have not realised until now that the mind will only sway and never still, the mind does not have a head or tail to move in a particular direction, it doesn't have a forward or reverse, you're wasting your life away. The mind doesn't even know its way.

To boost your self respect, you need to at first, observe your thinking. Some people are habitual thinkers. In being habitual, their thinking is patterned. It could be thinking of loss all the time, or creating fictitious imaginations of success in their space. Either way, such thinking is unproductive. So, firstly, observe your thinking. Observe how the thinking happens. What kinds of thoughts occur.

Do not reject any of the thoughts. They all belong to you. These are the thoughts you've nurtured until now. So, just observe them.

Thoughts Must Lead to Action

Observe what you do when your immediate family member calls you. Do you immediately respond to their call and actually go to them? Or, do you verbally respond to them that you are coming but think to yourself; I'll go to them after I finish what I am doing, and forget all about it? Action must follow your thinking. This is the second step to boost your self respect.

Let us take a broader example; Let us assume that you are driving on a street. After sometime, you encounter a traffic jam. What will you do? Will you sit in the car and blame the situation? Or, will you think aloud about what you can do to ease the jam? Your thinking supports and influences your attitude. Self Respect is an attitude.

The same attitude also holds good when you see something not right happening in your city, country or the world. If you claim to have a high sense of self respect, it'll show in the way you respond to local and national situations.

Integrate Thought Word and Action

The third step is to stitch together your thinking, speaking and action. This means, with the first step, conscious thinking will weed out random and unnecessary thoughts.

The second step will help you articulate your thinking. This brings in clarity in what you think. The third step is when you act on your thinking.

The three steps of thinking with awareness, articulating your thinking and actually acting on your thinking is the quickest way to boost your self respect.

Children have high self respect. They always think, articulate their thinking and follow up their thinking with action. They do this way because, children always live in the now moment.

How Do These Steps Boost Your Self Respect?

When your thoughts, words and actions follow one another, or are in synchronicity, then, there is no scope for the mind to sway. This way, you are always alert and aware. What you think is what you will speak. And what you speak is what you will act upon.

It is, in every which way, a commitment to yourself to stay in the present. Why don't you try it! When you apply what I have communicated you will see how this will boost your self respect.

Chapter - 10

4 Ways to Overcome Hurt Feelings

*You are given this life because you are
strong enough to live it.*

– Robin Sharma

This chapter addresses a few but very important questions we all have in our lives. What causes you to feel hurt? Why does it hurt when someone speaks or acts in ways you did not expect? Why do you feel that you are taken for granted? People don't understand your hurt feelings, why? How can you live with self respect, honour and dignity? How can you forgive and not remember your hurt feelings?

Did you know – One of the most important assets you must possess, nurture and nourish is self respect. Without self respect, you are simply incomplete. People you interact with you won't know how to perceive you, if you do not speak and act with self respect. Behaving without self respect can cause you to feel hurt.

What Is Self Respect?

According to the Oxford Dictionary, Self respect means that you behave with honour and dignity. While honour and respect means the same, dignity means – to be worthy of being you. Your dignity is, when you not only experience life, but, when you learn from your life experiences.

I have come across some people who want to make others happy. They go to any length without bothering about how they feel about themselves. Such people don't know that others don't understand their hurt feelings. They often make a fool of themselves. People like these are often taken for granted and feel hurt very easily. They act with emotion but without awareness. This is an example of behaving without honour and dignity. Furthermore, wanting to make others happy can make you physically ill, mentally weak and emotionally vulnerable.

Self respect means to live respecting your physical, mental and emotional existence which includes the body, and what you must use it for and mustn't. Respect the mind. Think possibilities. Think good about yourself and others. Encourage strengthening thoughts, discourage weakening or debilitating thoughts. Respect your emotions. Use your emotions to be compassionate towards others, to be loving towards all, to laugh more and be happy. People with healthy emotions do cry. However, they are strong within.

Help yourself first to be happy, loving and be content with what you are and what you have. Then help others in whatever way you can. Give your best. When situations demand, unknown strength emerges in your body, mind and your emotions. This is where you demonstrate your honour and dignity.

What Causes You to Feel Hurt?

When you are loving towards a person and that person doesn't reciprocate with love in the same way but, behaves in a way that is considered rude, you feel hurt.

Hurt feelings and attachment go hand in hand. The more attached you are to a person, the more easily you will feel hurt. Furthermore, As your attachment towards a person grows, your self respect declines. Then, you are more inclined to do anything to strengthen your attachment rather than behave with honour and dignity. People don't understand your hurt feelings. They can't. They care about what they get out of how you treat them.

Attachment Causes Hurt Feelings

You can get attached to a person who behaves with self respect. Have you witnessed this behaviour within your family and also in your corporate environment? We are all attracted to people who make others laugh and who themselves laugh more, isn't it? Attachment makes you hold onto the present that you are witnessing or experiencing. You can be attached to people or objects. You can also be attached to places and structures such as your house. Attachment makes you resist change. Attachment breeds as much fear as the hurt feelings it causes.

I knew of a person who was attached to her house that her father left for her. Her brother wanted to demolish the house and build an apartment. She wasn't aware of her brother's intentions. However, she was saving money to renovate and paint the house. When her brother approached her and forced her to sign on the papers, she felt so hurt that she had epileptic seizures. A few years later, unable to come to terms with her hurt feelings, she developed a brain tumour and passed away. Attachment weakens you.

I met a very strange family a few years ago. A lady married the man she was attracted and later very attached to, because he made everyone laugh. He loved having people around him. She told me that she dreamt, that if she married that man, then she will be always happy. What she realised after marrying this man is that, his behaviour wasn't real. He behaved funny because of his craving for importance. It turned out that he was in real, a very abusive person.

Possessiveness Can Hurt Both of You

A stronger form of attachment is possessiveness. Possessiveness happens when you become selfish and self centred and your motive is to control the other person to the maximum possible extent. When you become possessive about a person, your sense of like and dislike towards that person becomes very strong and you begin to enforce it on that person so that you can feel the pleasure of having the person with you all of the time. If that person reacts to your possessive behaviour with firmness, then, you are sure to feel hurt. In rare cases people turn suicidal. That behaviour is becoming more common these days.

Be Yourself

The first step to overcome your hurt feelings is to be real. Be real to yourself first. Observe your behaviour. Are you being unreal to yourself and to others? Being unreal can be very stressful. The real you is a loving, compassionate and happy being. That is what you did to anyone who held you in their arms when you were a tiny child. Back then, you did not know anything else apart from being real.

Do Not Change for Others

When you regain your ability to be yourself, do not change for anyone. Never compromise for others, no matter who they are and how close they are to you. There are people who will like you and those who won't. That's okay. If you get onto the business of making people to like you, you can join an acting class first. Actors successfully fake their personality on screen. I have heard in the past that some of the actors who acted mostly in villain roles were actually very gentle people in their real life.

Remember that people are always perceiving you. And they will take what they get from your behaviour and trust their perception. Every person you know in your life today, behaves with you, the way he or she has perceived you. People don't understand your hurt feelings. Don't waste time. So, be real.

I often tell people in relationships to keep their personality real. People often change their personality before marriage. They make promises that they can't keep.

And after marriage, the change drops off. You are back to being yourself because now you are safe to be you. Your spouse doesn't know who you are! Who was that person she was courting? Conflicts and hurt feelings arise because you changed from being you only because you wanted your partner to be your spouse.

Love Yourself

Being in love is the best feeling one can ever have. Always be in love with yourself. That's even better than being in love with someone else. It's not that people who are in love with themselves don't face problems. When you love yourself, you are happy, peaceful, ever ready to take on the different facets of life with the same zeal and enthusiasm.

I met a lady who didn't appreciate her body very much because she felt and looked out of shape. Only after she had parts of her skull scraped out because of a car accident and that left her head out of shape that she began to love herself. Don't be in love with your body. It keeps changing.

Loving yourself means to value your existence. You are invaluable. You, the sum total of your existence, is unique. When you set foot on this planet, your presence made this world a brighter place. Can you fathom this reality? Now, do everything possible to have this continue. When you love yourself, your contribution to the world multiplies manifold. You will not compromise, but you will give away what you love, in sacrifice. That is real freedom. Did you understand this? You won't, unless you live it. When you are in love, it shows. I have often spoken about meditation. If you have been hurt and want to get out of that feeling quickly, meditation really helps.

Forgive Always

This might seem very controversial. Most people I have met who speak of forgiveness do not know what that really means. Forgiveness has nothing to do with letting go of the other person!

Unforgiveness or the inability to forgive causes several chronic diseases and terminal illnesses. Unforgiveness comes from your inability to let go of expectations.

Forgiveness is a process to release your judgments and perceptions of the experiences you have had with the other person. Bear in mind that your perception with the person is bound by the experiences you have had with that person. So, you must release only experiences that have created your hurt feelings, hatred, anger, resentment, unhappiness, etc.

If you try to forgive someone for what they have done to you, you will actually feel more miserable than before.

Life has given me countless opportunities to learn to love, to be real to me and others and to always forgive. I followed these techniques for over 6 years and attained freedom from prejudice and perception. It is true that people don't understand your hurt feelings. They can't. The only way you can understand others is by understanding yourself. Be yourself, Love yourself and forgive always. This is the way to be happy always. My family and friends alike have been intrigued by the fact that nothing hurts me.

When you practice these techniques, you too will be free from hurt feelings.

Chapter - 11

Boost Your Self Worth

Self worth comes from one thing – thinking
that you are worthy.

– Wayne Dyer

Literally everyone is desiring and aspiring to be successful in life. And each one of us have a different version of success. I also have met people who want to be successful without knowing what success really means! However, most people haven't investigated what it takes to be successful. And running behind success can take a toll on your physical health, emotional stability and intellectual ability and agility, if you didn't get it right. There are literally countless gurus who are there to guide you to become successful. However, there aren't even a handful of those people who will tell you what internal work you need to do so that you can be driven towards success. That internal work might just be nurturing your self worth.

What Is Self Worth?

When I was a kid, I used to wonder, why is it that all creatures except for man, has everything for free while its only us who have to earn this thing called money to live! It is still a very pertinent question in many young minds and especially the ones who are unable to make sense of the connection between money and living.

Self worth, as the term itself, is self explanatory. It is the measure of your worthiness. Well! What does it exactly mean to someone who has no idea about worthiness?

The idea of self worth is rooted deeply in Ayurveda which has been adopted by the World Health Organisation. Health according to WHO says;

"A state of complete physical, mental and social well-being and not merely the absence of disease or infirmity."

WHO Constitution

Arriving to Physical, Mental and Social Well-being through Self Worth.

This is where it all begins. Self Worth enhances or depletes with how you conduct your life. It includes what you think, what you feel, what you speak and what actions you perform. It all depends on you. Well! How? Let's figure it out.

Let us start your day. At what time do you wake up? Come on, answer this question to yourself! What is your wake up time?

Now, here is the second question. Does your wake up time sustain your physical, emotional and intellectual health? If it does, then here is the next question. Does it also enhance your physical health, emotional stability and intellectual ability and agility? If no, then, does it deplete your physical health, emotional stability and intellectual ability and agility?

When you see that your waking up sustains or enhances your physical, emotional and intellectual health, you know that you are maintaining your self worthiness. Remember the WHO Constitution? It's not only about your physical health. It also includes your mental and emotional health. If your waking up time actually depletes your health, then, you need to change it.

What's a Good Wakeup Time?

According to Ayurveda, one must wake up before Sunrise. That constitutes good health and contributes to a continued state of good health.

Now, let us look at a thought you think. Do you often judge people? Do you often blame them, or have angry thoughts about them?

Once again, answer this question so you can get the clarity. Do these thoughts sustain, enhance or deplete your physical health, emotional stability and intellectual ability and agility?

Now, bring to your memory something you said. Again, ask yourself this question. Does my way of speaking sustain, enhance or deplete my physical health, emotional stability and intellectual ability and agility?

In the same way, you also need to investigate every action you perform and ask the question.

List of Activities That Support Your Self Worth

Listed here are some of the activities that support your Self Worth.

- Waking up before Sunrise

- Dedicated Meditation every morning

- Increasing physical endurance with early morning walk, jog, run

- Maintaining inner stability through Yoga

- Bathing everyday

- Scheduling your day healthily and actually working towards accomplishing the schedule you set for the day

- Nourishing your body with a healthy breakfast, healthy lunch and dinner, fruits and fresh fruit juices and all that makes your body feel light and energetic

- Commitment to time. Being there on time

- Working with perseverance, passion and dedication

- Completing daily tasks

- Connecting with family everyday

- Proper and appropriate communication

- Be open to learning

- Sharing and contributing to the well-being of fellow beings on this planet in your own way

- Invest your time laughing with family and friends everyday

- Retiring to bed early so you can start your next day early

List of Habits That Deplete Your Self Worth but Increase Your Self Importance

- Switching off alarm and continuing to sleep

- Lazing in bed

- Killing time indulging in social media such as Facebook, snapchat, WhatsApp and others

- Smoking

- Drinking alcohol

- Drug addiction

- Compulsive shopping online and offline

- Gossiping

- Indulging in sensual pleasure activities such as pornography

- Bad mouthing and blaming others

- Disrespecting others which includes your parents and relatives

- Procrastination

- Leaving tasks unfinished

- Convincing yourself that not completing a task is okay

Self Worth and Disciple

We all have heard of discipline. However, most of us don't know what it means. This is what I have been following. For me, discipline means to be a student or disciple of something you take up.

When you take up disciplining your Self Worth, you are a student of Self Worth. You constantly observe every thought you think, every word you speak and every act you perform and constantly and consistently modify yourself in every which way so that you enhance your physical health, emotional stability and intellectual ability and agility.

In the Indian scriptures, we call it Swadhyaya or Self Study.

Self Worth and Health

People who often work for money are victims to high blood pressure, diabetes and a host of other health problems. On the other hand, people who work with passion are the ones who enhance their physical health, emotional stability and intellectual ability and agility.

Women who expect their husbands to love them also fall victims to low self worth. Women must enhance their self worth by taking care of their physical health, emotional stability and intellectual ability and agility by leading a meaningful life full of self acceptance, and appreciation for oneself, rather than expecting their spouse and in-laws to accept and appreciate them.

When people come to me, I coach them specifically so that they are able to overcome their personal and professional challenges through specifically designed treatments and therapies that release your mind blocks and help you walk out of your self created prison of impossibilities into a world of possibilities.

Those who have chosen to work with themselves have rediscovered their enthusiasm and passion for life.

This Is How She Regained Her Self Worth

I remember a lady whom I had to work with while I was coaching doctors to Learn Nadi Pariksha in Haryana. This lady was depressed because she felt her husband was not giving her importance. The husband and son were both doctors. They had shown her to several doctors. She also was on anti-depressants and yet, she had not recovered. She had fungal infections on her body.

When I approached her, she was constantly murmuring; "I want to die." I went to her bedside, gave her a session of Marma Chikitsa and asked her to get up. When she didn't, I began mocking her in Hindi saying; "She's just acting."

I did this for two days. And surprisingly, on the third day, she got up on her own, washed herself clean and served me hot Paranthas.

I am in touch with the family. Even today, 11 years after that episode, she is going strong. Her husband has passed on though!

Your self worth is a determining factor of your physical health, emotional stability and intellectual ability and agility. Maintaining your Self Worth can go a long way in living a good life and setting an example to so many others who look up to you.

Chapter - 12

Boost Your Self Confidence

Passion is energy. Feel the power that comes from focussing on what excites you.

– Oprah Winfrey

Everyone wants to be confident. However, few know the actual meaning of being confident and how to believe in oneself. When you have self confidence, you feel sure about your abilities, qualities, or ideas. Being self-confident is a mark of self assurance. Self assurance is largely built up by ones self-respect. Self-confidence begins with treating yourself well. The opposite of it is the lack of confidence. Lack of self-confidence causes weight gain, depression, anxiety and stress and several other diseases and illnesses. People with low self-confidence often complain more. They see more problems and do not look to solve challenges. They feel stuck. Self-confidence is a mental state. It can be cultivated.

5 Steps to Being Self Confident Now

Self-confidence means to recognise yourself and treat yourself well. You have often heard motivational speakers say; that you are unique and that there is not a second you on this planet. It does give you a motivational boost when you listen to them. That definitely makes you feel better. However you did not have a practice that can keep you in that state of thought and feeling. So, the question is, what can I do to keep my self-confidence and self-respect high? So, here are the 5 steps to being self-confident now.

Own Responsibility

The first step is to accept responsibility. None of us like where we are for long! We want to move forward and be better than what we are today. But, dislike won't take you further. It will only make you feel more miserable. Remember, self-confidence is all about the journey. It's not only about getting there.

Taking responsibility for where I am at this moment is the first step to being self-confident. You are here because of the choices you made. Don't like this place, make new choices.

Did you know that what you think and feel causes a vibrational shift in your being-ness and affects every little or large thing in this Universe? This is real. Everything you think and feel does cause a shift. If something awesome or awful happens somewhere, may be your thought triggered that happening! Don't just brush it off. Believe it for now so that, when your mind has shifted from your current space, you'll know just how powerful your thoughts and feelings are. So, your first step is to accept responsibility for what you think and feel.

I'd like to share something experience of how your thoughts and feelings actually manifest.

What You Think Happens for Real

A few years ago, my wife and I were traveling in our car. As I turned into a street, we found the tar on the road neatly laid. It was such a beautiful experience to drive on that road. My wife blurted; now you'll see, they will dig up this road for some repair work. I retorted saying; why did you make such a statement? Don't you know your thoughts can actually manifest?

A couple of hours later we turned into the same street. All of a sudden, my wife held her head between her hands. I didn't know what was happening. I asked my wife if she was okay. The street had quite a bit of traffic. When the traffic cleared, I could understand my wife's actions. The tar had been broken into and the road was indeed being dug.

You just don't know how powerful your thoughts are. So, accept responsibility for what you think and feel.

Ask and It Is Given

Most of us don't ask! We believe life is like this. It does not have to be. When you step into a lift, you need to press the button to go somewhere. Until you press the button, the lift won't move. Or else, if someone else presses a button on the inside or outside, the lift will go to where that someone wants it to go. It is your responsibility to ask. Well, whom to ask may be your next question. There is no one outside of you whom you need to ask. Everything happens on the inside. So, who's inside? [whisper] The real you.

Do you realise your true ability? You are so smart that while you were being born, you created not just this body! You divided yourself into forces that will assist you in whatever you do. This was the amount of self-respect you demonstrated. These forces are dormant now because you haven't used them. This seems weird or absurd right? Think for a moment. How did inventions happen? What forces helped the inventors? Something more than what they believed there were was assisting them, right? No one made it by luck. People received favours because they asked for it.

Let me warn you! Getting everything you ask for is not how it works! So, just ask for what you need and it will happen. Yes! It is the law of attraction. There's a way to go about it.

Plan Your Journey

It is important to plan your journey. When you plan your journey you must pay attention a critical fact. Every thought you think will produce a consequence. And you have no clue what it is until it actually happens. So, there are possibilities that your plan may not happen as you wanted it to. Therefore, keep your plan and be ready for adjustments and modifications keeping your goal in sight.

Act on It Now

Wherever you are, to shift, you need to move internally in your thoughts and your actions. You need to do it when you decided to. Never procrastinate. Never give up. Keep exploring. Opportunities never cease. To be self-confident you need to act now. This doesn't mean when you miss one opportunity, another will come. You have to choose your opportunity. Know that, every success story has a struggle behind it. I am not asking you to struggle but, you must act when you decided to. Take one step at a time. Every action will produce a result. The result will tell you whether the action steps you took were appropriate or not. Keep going as long as it is taking you towards your goal. When you notice something is wrong, stop, investigate and take corrective action and continue acting. Remember to ask for assistance when you need to.

Consistency

Whatever you do, be consistent. Most people who claim to lack self-confidence give up too quickly. For all you know, you might just be near the curve that will trigger transformation in your journey. If you give up then, don't blame anyone else for it. Consistency brings change. Practicing the same thing over and over again creates a habit. To change your old habits of procrastination or delayed action, you must begin that change by acting now and staying consistent with your journey. Everyone is born self-confident and with self-respect. It's what you do after that, that matters.

The journey is never difficult. Your thinking and feeling makes it difficult. For people who are driven internally, the journey is always something to look forward to. Journeys bring with them rich experiences and tons of learning. That's what makes you grow. So, get prepared, and begin the journey you have been wanting, to be self-confident now. Practice the 5 steps to be self confidence now.

Chapter - 13

Overcome Procrastination

The most effective way to do it
Is to do it.

– Amelia Earhart

Procrastination is the science of inaction by postponing an activity that needs your attention now. People often procrastinate because they can have the pleasure of not doing anything. Self importance is a big threat to your job, career and your mental and physical wellbeing if procrastination is what you love to indulge in everyday. Procrastination is potentially hazardous to your mental well being. It causes you to find reasons to stay in your comfort zone and you will begin to blame situations, people and the company itself for your indecision. The habit is self defeating. Stop procrastinating before it consumes your mental and physical health.

What Happens When You Procrastinate?

When tasks look like they are piled up, you want a break from your routine. That's fine. But, what if that routine becomes the main lookout instead of keeping your mind busy in accomplishing your tasks? That's when you begin procrastinating.

In the beginning, your procrastination is extremely pleasurable because this is a new habit and the pile of tasks you choose to work on later is small. However, as the habit kicks in, you see the tasks pile up. Looking at the list of unfinished tasks causes you to postpone it further. In the beginning you were procrastinating because you wanted a break. Now, you want to run away from the pile of tasks because they seem just too much for you to handle.

This is what procrastinating does to you. It causes you to dwell in self importance. Self importance makes you mentally sick. You feel more anxious and less inclined to find a solution. Instead, you begin to look at problems and people to blame for the situation you are in. Any person who is willing to help you come out of your problem will have to give up their time to listen to your reasons and complaints. Psychiatrists usually prescribe anti-depressants or medications to control anxiety. You do not need any anti-depressants or anxiety medication. What you need is an air of self confidence and there are just 4 steps to stop procrastination and get back to life.

4 Steps to Stop Procrastination

There are just 4 steps to stop procrastination. Following these steps will ensure that your life will transform within a week for your best.

Make a List but Keep It Small and Easy

One of the most important tasks to stop procrastinating is to begin writing a list. However, there is a caution for you. Don't bring your guilt into this activity. Often guilt causes you to put all the unfinished task in one list. One glance at your list and it'll defeat your purpose.

So, keep your list small with current tasks that you need to accomplish.

Self Talk

Talking to yourself to motivate yourself to get up and do the tasks is a good way to begin. You can begin by talking to yourself saying; "I know I want to rest now but, I must do this task now. It will benefit me the most."

Get up and Get to Work

Once your list is ready and your self talk is done, it is time for action. You must be quick. Get to action with your tasks now. There is nothing like getting up and doing your tasks. When you have accomplished, the pleasure of completing your tasks is way too rewarding. I wouldn't want to give that up for anything!

In my teens, my father tried waking me up at 5:30 a.m. every morning. Those were the worst days when you want to sleep but your father will come and wake you up. And my father would simply pull the sheets off me and make the situation so uncomfortable that I had to get out of bed.

Several years later, when I had grownup, my father left it to me. For a few years, I woke up whenever I wanted to.

Then one day, I decided, enough was enough. Now, I want to wake up every morning at 4:30 a.m. I needed a mantra to wake up early. I searched everywhere but couldn't find one. Everyone I asked told me, "Just do it."

So, I thought to myself, 4:30 a.m. doesn't come after 4:30 a.m. That is reason enough for me to wake up at 4:30 a.m. Today, I don't need an alarm. I just wake up at 4:30 a.m. and I'm off for a great day.

Learn Your Lesson

The most important part of accomplishing your tasks is about learning the lesson. When you accomplished your task, you feel proud. You feel you are on the top of your world. All that is fine. To be successful, your continuity counts. It's not a one time activity. You need to be at it. If you learnt this lesson, you will never procrastinate. That lesson must come from your experience of getting into the continuity of accomplishing tasks and celebrating your achievement.

When you have learnt the lesson, you don't need the first 3 steps. If you haven't learnt your lesson, then you are bound to fail again.

It is not so difficult to stop procrastination! Neither is staying up to date continually with your tasks and schedules. And that challenge can be rewarding only when you reward yourself with yet another accomplishment.

Chapter – 14

The Mythical Me Time

Everybody has the same amount of time during the day. You can either spend your time or invest your time.

– Chip Kelly

People are generally frustrated with each other and they look for sometime away from everyone. They call it ME time. The first time I heard ME time was several years ago when someone casually mentioned to me; "I just want to spend time with myself. I want some ME time." We all have 24 hours to ourselves everyday. How do you want to spend these 24 hours is all that really matters. That, indeed is the real ME time.

The 24 hours available with me today, from the morning, is my time. How I live the 24 hours and what I do with these 24 hours is all that matters.

How weird this ME time is! Did you know that the 24 hours I have with me, is all my time? The 24 hours available with you today, from the morning, is really your time and that is all that you have today. So, everyone alive on this planet, at this moment, is living their 24 hours right now. How you live the 24 hours and what you do with these 24 hours is all that matters.

What Makes You Want Me Time?

What on earth makes you want more time on hand than what you already have? And what are you doing with the time you have with you?

Most people I know who want the ME time do not have a count on where their time goes! You are accountable for your time. No one else is. So, you need to be really stingy when it comes to spending your time. This means, you need to be really choosy about whom you are spending your time with. It is this lack of accountability for your time that makes you want more time for yourself – the ME time.

Be Accountable for Your Time

Are you keeping track of your time? Where you are spending it and what are you spending it for?

Just like you count every little bit of money you have, it is important for you to count every second too. You must be accountable for your time because that is your time. More importantly, that is all the time you have for today. With every second spent, your time is less by that much today. If you throw it away carelessly, you can't have it back. It is gone for ever. That's why, you need to be extremely careful about time.

Value for your time increases or decreases with how you use your time and to what use you put your time.

What Are You Using Your Time For?

You alone are responsible for how you use your time. Value for your time increases or decreases with how you use your time and to what use you put your time. When you value time, it boosts your self confidence. Activities that can enhance value for time.

- Invest your time in family

- Reading is an excellent habit to invest time in regularly

- Reflect on an idea and bring it to life

- Meditate regularly

- Keep your meetings tight and crisp. Do not throw away your time in meaningless talk

- Economise on time with better productivity at work

Beware of Multi Tasking

Multi tasking is a mania that has gripped the world. People who multi task often have a lot to do. That's because, when they multi-task, they actually are all over the place and they are never really done. They have their hands in 10 different things and a little of everything gets done and nothing ever gets accomplished. It is actually slower and that means, it takes longer than, when you focus on one task at a time. There are a marginal few who know how to focus and get more done in less time. That's an art.

When you decide to be happy and successful, all you have to do is use your time cautiously and for the right reasons. Do not throw your time away carelessly. Time is God. Time is money. It is everything.

Chapter - 15

Be Casual but Not Careless

*When you are careless with other people, you bring
ruin upon yourself.*

– Jenny Lind

Every personal relationship demands two commitments
from the partners. That the partners must be casual and
committed. Being casual means to be easy going and not
being serious. Being careless means to stop investing in
your relationship. You let your relationship off guard,
off the hook. Let us learn how to be casual and never be
careless.

Very often, partners become serious and dampen their
relationships with compromises and arguments. What is more
dangerous is when you become careless.

In the beginning of any relationship, there is attachment,
communication and reciprocation. However, as time passes,
an attitude of carelessness sets in. Your self worth and self
respect do not matter any longer. You can behave as you like.

You can quarrel, fight and create an ugly scene, whenever your mood demands so.

Why Be Casual?

When you are casual in a relationship, you are never worked up. You find solutions to challenges. You are always in the mood. Those who were courting couples before marriage would know what I am talking.

A man's goal ends with marriage whereas a woman's life begins with marriage. Men need to understand that life begins with marriage. It's not that your mother stopped taking care of you and your wife will do it from now and onwards. This careless attitude is what works up a woman's nerves.

When you get married, be enthusiastic. You now have someone to share your joys with. But, remember, if your partner believes he or she is your remote control, practice staying out of control. Life offers many ways of overcoming challenges. The best way is to switch off, or mute your hearing when it sounds harsh. But, don't stop at that. Find out what caused your partner to become harsh and act on them.

The Cost of Being Careless

When you are careless in a relationship, it usually comes at a huge cost. Carelessness costs your relationship. The ship rocks. Yes! That's right.

Men, when they meet their could be or would be life partner, throw an attitude that's unreal. They know that they have to project their best impression. Remember, "first impression is best impression"? However, after marriage, all the drama stops. No more impressing. Let's chill.

A woman takes your attitude in her first meeting for real and that's where all the trouble begins. When you let go of the unreal for the real, she doesn't know you. She will feel such insecurity in her.

One lady came to me for a consultation because she felt her life had no meaning. She was married for just 4 years. Her husband was okay in the beginning. A few months after marriage, he had taken to playing poker and he occasionally smoked pot. Such was his indulgence that he had asked his wife not to disturb him. Such carelessness can wreak havoc in your life.

What could be worse! Your spouse could fall off into someone else's ship and sail away, leaving your relationship torn apart.

Maintaining a Casual Attitude

Any marriage is beautiful when you add three ingredients into it. They are; be real, have fun and throw in surprises. These three ingredients can create magic in your relationship.

Every person has to discover what fun elements you need to bring into your relationship and what surprises you will throw in. There are no manuals and no formulae. Invent your own. Be real. Do not splurge money when you don't have it. Do not borrow money to make your spouse happy. Money cannot buy happiness. It's true.

Saying the Magic Words Isn't Enough

It's not enough if you say how much you love your spouse. What is important is how much you value yourself. When you value yourself, you will do everything that needs to be done so that your relationship is as fresh as the morning dew. I suggest you read this line again. This is different from doing anything that makes your spouse happy. Never do anything to make your spouse happy. Effort is important. Result is not.

There are no holidays to a married person. You must not need one. Just keep your relationship filled with fun and surprises so that your life is worth it.

Chapter – 16

Love It All

Love is... The only thing you get more of by giving it away.

– Tom Wilson

Love is possibly the most used word and yet the most misunderstood in human evolution. People have been less loving towards each other and more transactional in every sense. But they still choose to call it love. Love is not transactional. It cannot be lost. Love cannot be gained either. Love is life. It is love because of which you and I are born. You do not need gifting ideas to get love.

On valentine's day all hell breaks loose. All the mess happens. When everyone falls from love to what they want to recognise as love.

What Is Love?

Love is an expression of the Self to the Self. Wait, let me explain this jargon. Let's say you want to buy your friend a gift. You go into a store to purchase a gift. You see all the gifting ideas presented in the store. The first thing you'd do when you are standing in front of the rack where gifts are showcased is, think about your friend and what choices your friend would prefer and appreciate. As you are thinking, you feel happiness. You feel love. That feeling is from you to yourself. That same feeling does not arise when you are with your friend. That feeling is different because heaps of expectations are between both of you. That is a transaction. Transaction cannot be love.

Love has no expectations. Love flows freely. When it's love, it shows. The only way you can feel more love is when it is shared without expecting anything in return. Love is health. Love is healing.

So, How Does Love Work?

When two friends meet, its love flowing from you, through your friend and back to you. It is flowing from you and to you. When that happens, the mind misinterprets it as; "My friend loves me," or "My friend feels love for me." You cannot feel anything that's outside of you. Remember this truth. You cannot feel another person's feelings inside you. Yes, you can feel something happening within! That's because these feelings exist in you.

What about the Physicality of Love?

The body experiences changes when love blossoms. When you address these physical feelings such as hugging or kissing, then, love dies. That action of hugging or kissing is an expression of physical feelings of your attraction and attachment towards the other person. If it is driven towards a sexual intent, then it is lust. Definitely not love.

How Can I Love Then?

Love is not something you do! Love is who you are. Again, this needs simplification. Have you held an infant in your hands? What does the infant do to you that you feel happy and want to hug the child? Nothing, right? That infant doesn't do anything for you to feel so nice. You feel so good, just like that! That infant is living love. And that's what you were when you were born. You simply don't remember.

You don't have to love. When you care, love expresses itself. Being compassionate, is an expression of love. Helping others without any expectation is an expression of love. You are doing it because that's what you feel like doing. Love has no motive for its expression. But, the moment you have a motive or an expectation from what flows through you, love dies.

Does That Mean the World Is Wrong in Loving Each Other?

When you look at a mirror, whom do you see? Is it you or your reflection? And when you appreciate whom you see in the mirror, do you appreciate yourself or your reflection? The mind tells you that you love your reflection. In reality, you are loving yourself through the reflection. When you get habituated to standing in front of the mirror to look at yourself so that you can appreciate yourself, you can no longer love yourself without a mirror.

Now, replace the mirror with a person. The same thing happens. When you don't spend time with yourself, you need someone else to appreciate you, accept you and pay attention to you so that you can feel more comfortable. The world is driven by this reflection.

How Can I Love Myself?

That's a good question. I will show you how you can love yourself now. Can you use your mirror now? Ok. You can stand in front of the mirror if it's long, else, just let the mirror be in front of you so that you can see your face in it.

Self Love

Now, imagine that you are holding a flower with your hands in front of your chest. It can be any flower of any colour. Observe whether this flower is a bud, has blossomed or has wilted (is dull and will whither away). Order this flower to come into full bloom.

We will now breathe in love and breathe out love, ok! You can do this practice with your eyes open or closed. I prefer to do this practice with closed eyes. This is one of the best gifting ideas I have for you.

Breathe…

As you breathe in, tell yourself; I am breathing in love. Feel the breath enter your chest through the flower. Next, as you breathe out, tell yourself; I direct this love to my reflection. Do this a few times, say 15 times. Watch what happens every time you breathe in love and every time you direct this love to your reflection.

I'd like to give a small tip here so that you can feel more love. Every time you breathe in, increase the number of flowers. Let 1 flower become 2 flowers. Then 2 flowers can become 10. Like this, go on increasing the number of flowers you will hold between your hands. During this practice, I imagine that I have about 500 flowers.

At the end of 15 breaths, watch how you feel. Look at yourself in the mirror. Do you see a lovelier you? A more beautiful or more handsome you? This is the way to love yourself. If you want to expand this love, share these imaginary flowers with your wife. Imagine her standing in front of you instead of seeing yourself in the mirror. Be nice to her. Be nice to your parents, your brothers and sisters. Do something nice today and every day. When you are love, you can be more loving towards your family. That's the way to love. That's the only way to love. And that is the only way to let your wife have what she really wants.

To explore more of his work please check his website:

https://maheshkrishnamurthy.com

RECOMENDACIONES PARA SIETE MARCAS DE UNA IGLESIA NEO-TESTAMENTARIA

De ves en cuando se necesita ver la iglesia neotestamentaria para compararle con nuestras iglesias de hoy. Dave Black nos ha dado esa vista en su libro Siete marcas de una iglesia neotestamentaria. En una manera bíblica y clara nos hace ver la manera en que la iglesia neotestamentaria actua, y nos pone un modelo bíblico para nuestras iglesias. Aquí se encuentra lo más básica de la iglesia de Cristo, y nos ayuda para establecer y crecer iglesias bíblicas. Lo recomiendo como un libro principal para los que estamos como pastores y líderes du Su santa iglesia.

Alex Montoya
Pastor de First Fundamental Bible Church, Whittier, CA

En estos días cuando la iglesia muchas veces se ha convertido a un centro de diversión, es muy importante de revisar las siete marcas básicas de la iglesia que vemos en Hechos 2, 37–47. Este libro es fácil de entender con muchos ejemplos personales. Lo recomendó para estudio bíblico de grupos Cristianos en todas iglesias.

Dra. Aida Besançon Spencer
Profesora del Nuevo Testamento,
Gordon-Conwell Theological Seminary

Creo que es justo decir que conozco al hermano David Black. Él ha sido mi profesor, y he sido uno de sus pastores. En un viaje a Etiopía, recuerdo preguntándole a su esposa (Becky), "¿Cuáles son las fortalezas de Dr. Black?" Ella respondió, "Ver el panorama en grande y hacerlo simple de una manera que todos puedan entender." Siete marcas de una iglesia neotestamentaria es tal libro. Claro, conciso, interesante, y lleno de sabiduría celestial que revolverá su corazón y mente para desear "evangelio-madurez" para la gloria de Cristo.

Dr. Jason Evans
Pastor, Bethel Hill Baptist Church

Justo cuando pensaba que había leído mi libro favorito escrito por Dave Black, ¡sale este libro! Sin importar sí Dios lo ha salvado recientemente o sí usted ha estado caminando con Jesús por muchos años, este libro es para ti. Jesús dijo en Mateo 16, 18, "Edificaré mi iglesia". Desde la perspectiva de Jesús, la iglesia era futuro, era su posesión, y él fue su arquitecto. Hoy en día, estamos tentados a olvidar sus principios, verla como posesión de otra persona, y construirla con las manos y mentes humanas. En segundo lugar a una visión equivocada del evangelio, nada puede afectar la gran Comisión más que una visión equivocada de la iglesia. Siete marcas de una iglesia neotestamentaria es un necesario recordatorio que nosotros somos una iglesia que necesita "hacer iglesia" en términos de Dios, y no nuestros. Yo he sido beneficiado enormemente de esta estudio cuidadoso de Hechos 2, 37–47. Créanme cuando digo, no podemos permitirnos descuidar estos once versículos si esperamos ver este mundo cambiado para Dios "hacia abajo" en nuestros días (Hechos 17, 6).

Thomas W. Hudgins, PhD, EdD
Capital Seminary and Graduate School, Washington, D.C.

¡Bueno, David Black lo ha hecho otra vez! En su libro Siete marcas de una iglesia neotestamentaria él trae a la luz el hecho de que mucho de lo que se está haciendo en nuestras iglesias del siglo XXI no tiene poco o ningún parecido con lo que enseña la Biblia. ¡Ay! ¡Pero es cierto! Dave nos llama para echar un vistazo a cómo "hacer iglesia" y tratar de traer reforma. No es que hemos elegido ser desobediente o antibíblicos en una manera intencional. Sin embargo, al igual que las mareas del océano, que comen un castillo de arena, verdades bíblicas están siendo erosionados por tradiciones